CEDAW and the legitimacy of misogynous religious institutions.
Re-readings in canonical Hindu *shastras*.

I0171191

TAPATI BHARADWAJ

Copyright © 2016 Lies and Big Feet. Readers of these articles may copy them without the copyright owner's permission, if the author and publisher are acknowledged in the copy and copy is used for educational, not-for-profit purposes.

All rights reserved.

ISBN: 9384281018
ISBN-13: 978-9384281014

CONTENTS

SECTION I:
INTRODUCTION.

1 INTRODUCTION.

The Convention on the Elimination of All Forms of Discrimination against Women (CEDAW) was adopted in 1979 by the UN General Assembly, and can be seen as an international bill of rights for women. All countries that have accepted the Convention are compelled to follow up with a series of measures that would end all forms of discrimination against women. Any country that has ratified or acceded to the Convention, is legally and morally obliged to ensure that women are not discriminated against, or oppressed.

If the purpose of CEDAW is to end all acts of discrimination against women by organizations, then we would be compelled to include organizations that propagate religion in the public domain as mostly and often, these religious bodies propound theology that is comfortably couched in misogyny, thereby validating a heightened sense of machismo as being endemic to human behaviour. Undoubtedly and what is obvious is that any nation that is a participant to CEDAW is legally bound to examine and interrogate the role that is played by these religious organizations in normalising misogyny and in also disseminating these ideas in the public domain on a daily basis.

Feminist scholars can cry themselves hoarse in trying to understand the nature of institutionalised misogyny that permeates all aspects of civil, social and religious life and has been seen as the status quo since times immemorial. On similar lines, development theorists and economists have tried to address how poverty works in order to alleviate it. But if we refuse to acknowledge that religion which is the bedrock of all societies- is the perpetrator in enabling this kind of gender-class oppression – then it is a losing battle that feminists and economists wage as they analyse the origins of social inequalities.

Within the Indian context, any institution/organization that propagates the Hindu religious texts – is complicit in acts of perpetuating misogyny in an institutionalised manner. Why is it that feminists and economists and development scholars never analyse how these religious institutions work in creating a social order which entrenches misogyny in the psyche of all citizens? If India is a signatory to CEDAW, should not the nation also ensure that all organizations – religious and secular – be not involved in any form of discrimination against women?

WITHIN A NON HINDU CONTEXT.

All countries which are signatories to CEDAW are legally bound to adhere to its rules that aim towards undoing all oppressive and discriminatory practises against women. The implication is that no institution – secular or religious – can propound and propagate any misogyny ridden dictums (theological or otherwise) in the public domain.

If we consider how religious institutions of Christianity and Islam continue with propagating theology which in no way attempts to undo the underlying misogyny that permeates all aspects of these religious institutions – then we are compelled to question as to why these realms of religion are never interrogated

If a country is a signatory to CEDAW, then the Judiciary of that nation is legally bound to closely monitor the nature of what happens in the domain of religion, and what exactly are these religious institutions propagating. It would be erroneous to conflate the theological aspects of those religions with what would essentially comprise temporal social modes of being that are also seen as comprising "revealed knowledge". Religious authorities need to be chastised by the Judiciary of all the nations that are signatories to CEDAW as they propound theology that does not interrogate the underlying misogyny. Subsequently, these religious institutions need to rewrite these canonical religious texts ensuring that the flagrant misogyny is erased; not doing so would be a legal misdemeanour as it would comprise a violation of CEDAW.

DO RELIGIOUS INSITUTIONS VIOLATE THE CONSTITUION OF INDIA?

One of the fundamental rights that is granted to all citizens of India is the Right to Freedom of Religion, which is Article 25 in the Constitution of India. I quote at lengths to validate my point:

> Article 25. Freedom of conscience and free profession, practice and propagation of religion.-
>
> (1) Subject to public order, morality and health and to the other provisions of this Part, all persons are equally entitled to freedom of conscience and the right freely to profess, practise and propagate religion.
>
> (2) Nothing in this article shall affect the operation of any existing law or prevent the State from making any law.

(a) regulating or restricting any economic, financial, political or other secular activity which may be associated with religious practice;

(b) providing for social welfare and reform or the throwing open of Hindu religious institutions of a public character to all classes and sections of Hindus.

If we closely examine 2 (b), we can arrive at the obvious conclusion that the State can make laws that throw "open" Hindu religious institutions of a public character to all classes and section of Hindus. If we take this as a basic premise that is granted to us by the Constitution, then we can also argue that simply throwing open the doors of "religious institutions" is not enough and we need to scrutinise what exactly is propounded and propagated within the walls of these "religious institutions of a public nature"; it is one thing when these religious institutions talk about God and the Supreme Being and the Hindu *shastras,* and it is also another thing when these institutions also throw in a lot of theology which is outright misogynous and sexist and caste-ist, and thereby excludes half the population of India. Are religious institutions participants in propounding sexist and caste-ist theology which affects how people engage in their every-day lives? Do these institutions therefore, violate the Fundamental Rights that are granted to all the citizens of India by the Constitution.

Moreover, if such caste-ist and sex-ist discourse is allowed to function in the public realm, it tantamounts to being unconstitutional and comprises a violation of one of the Fundamental Rights that has been granted in India, namely, Article15 of the Constitution of India and is the Right to Equality.

Article 15. Prohibition of discrimination on grounds of religion, race, caste, sex or place of birth.-

(1) The State shall not discriminate against any citizen on grounds only of religion, race, caste, sex, place of birth or any of them.

(2) No citizen shall, on grounds only of religion, race, caste, sex, place of birth or any of them, be subject to any disability, liability, restriction or condition with regard to-

(a) access to shops, public restaurants, hotels and places of public entertainment; or

(b) the use of wells, tanks, bathing *ghats*, roads and places of public resort maintained wholly or partly out of State funds or dedicated to the use of the general public.

(3) Nothing in this article shall prevent the State from making any special provision for women and children.

The fact that religious institutions often and always propagate misogyny ridden social dictums and equate them with notions of Existence and Hindu theology, makes us question the constitutional validity of the practise, as it is a flagrant violation of Article 15, which aims towards undoing all discriminatory practises.

The larger question which we should all strive towards is: why should the Hindu *shastras* be seen as comprising, in its totality, "revealed knowledge" when large chunks of it refer to temporal behavior that is based on one's gender or caste (the most oft-cited being *Manusmriti's Varnashrama*). Why are they cited as being infallible when often these texts propound extremely sexist and caste-ist views?

The yet unresolved conundrum, thus is: how does the Indian state (which is also a signatory to CEDAW) allow these texts to be a part of public discourse as they are often, and mostly, quite unconstitutional? The rampant sexist and caste-ist discourse that is intrinsic to our Hindu *shastras* is overt and unapologetic.

THE NEED TO INITIATE AN EPISTEMIC CHANGE TO ALLOW FOR PARITY FOR WOMEN.

The Indian Constitution in 1947, declared equality as a Fundamental Right. It also guaranteed equal protection under the law, provided equal opportunities in public employment, and prohibited discrimination in public places. Equality was constructed as being accessible to all and did not take into account that each individual, being located within different social realities, was not similarly positioned to enact this concept. This rhetoric, which existed at the discursive level, did not affect women materially. The Indian Government's commitment to equality was seriously challenged and critiqued in 1974 when *Towards Equality: Report of the Committee on the Status of Women in India,*[1] a report on the status of women, was published. In 1971, the Ministry of Education and Social Welfare had appointed a committee "to examine the constitutional, legal and administrative provisions that have a bearing on the social status of women, their education and employment" and to assess the impact of these provisions. The research and it's publication was also, partly, in response to a United Nations request to all countries to prepare reports on the status of women for International Women's Year, scheduled for 1975.[11] The report concluded by stating that women's status had not improved since Independence, and is worth quoting at length:

> Social structures, cultural norms, and value systems influence social expectations regarding the behavior of both men and women, and determine a woman's

---

[1] *Towards Equality: Report of the Committee on the Status of Women in India.* New Delhi: Govt. of India, Ministry of Education & Social Welfare, Dept. of Social Welfare, 1974.

role and her position in society to a great extent. The most important of these institutions are the systems of descent, family and kinship, marriage, and religious traditions: ... The normative standards do not change at the same pace as changes in other forms of social organization brought about by such factors as technological and educational advance, urbanization, increasing populations.. .This gap explains the frequent failure of law and educational policy to produce the desired effect on social attitudes.[2]

In this report to the government of India, the members of the committee, concluded by recommending (amongst other things) "establishment of women's *panchayats* at the village level with autonomy and resources of their own for the management and administration of welfare and development programs."[3] This issue was also problematised by numerous female legislators and feminist activists.

Even if women are given parity in the realm of the polity

---

[2] Ibid. pp. 114-115.

[3] Ibid., pp. 114-115.

and the state, would the value systems and the cultural standards change? The system of "religious tradition" was mentioned as being a root cause that contributed to maintaining the cultural values, but no means were mentioned in the report that would systematically address ways to undo these value systems. If, as the report *Towards Equality* stated, a "woman's role and her position in society" in India is determined by cultural values which in turn are defined by "religious traditions," then we have to examine the nature of these religious institutions; interrogating the Hindu *shastras* will allow us to conclude that they are incredibly sex-ist and caste-ist in nature and unconstitutional.

How we, that is, women – eat, breathe, dress and conduct ourselves and the kinds of labor that we are allowed to perform – are codified and seen as intrinsic to the Hindu *shastras*. The realm of religion, indeed, is the privilege of men. And indeed, it would not be salacious to argue that self-identifying Brahmin men and those who function in the religious institutions and are the so-called custodians of Hindu *dharma* are mostly myopic; they are unable to distinguish between what constitutes "revealed knowledge" about Existence and Brahman and Creation, and temporal gender-caste based social modes of being. What prevents the government of India (which is also a signatory to CEDAW) from slapping legal cases against these religious institutions as they propound unconstitutional rhetoric that, in all respects, violates our Fundamental Rights that are embedded within the Indian Constitution?

Methodology of Reading.

I have selected certain sections from *Manusmriti* and the *Adhyatma Ramayana* and engaged with these texts to enable for a dialectics to emerge; the text is therefore, juxtaposed with analysis which questions a few of the basic assumptions. This is a kind of a dialogue which will take place and there is no perfect right answer.

Often, these texts articulate ideas that, if believed implicitly and absolutely, are unconstitutional. As these ideas coexist alongside religious belief systems which talk about Brahman and Creation, they are interrogated and the theological aspects are separated from those sections that refer to social behavior.

SECTION II:
EXTRACTS FROM THE
MANUSMRITI.

2 RE-READING THE *MANUSMRITI*[4]

If we refuse to accept the constructed nature of the Hindu *shastras* and assume them as being infallible – as these texts comprise "revealed knowledge," then we take a myopic view of the fact that the *mantras* on Being and Brahman cannot be equated on the same spectrum with the misogyny that is also located as being a-historical. These texts on Hinduism are part of the everyday discourse that function in the public realm of both the secular and the religious. We need to be able interrogate the nature of these religious texts and conceptualise new methodologies of reading. Doing so will allow us to separate that which is "revealed knowledge" from that which is basically outright misogyny and comments upon temporal social behaviours.

---

[4] All references from *Manusmriti* are from Georg Búhler's *The Laws of Manu*, Oxford: Clarendon Press, 1886.

EXTRACTS FROM CHAPTER 1:

1. The great sages approached Manu, who was seated with a collected mind, and, having duly worshipped him, spoke as follows:

2. 'Deign, divine one, to declare to us precisely and in due order the sacred laws of each of the (four chief) castes (*varna*) and of the intermediate ones.

3. 'For thou, O Lord, alone knowest the purport, (i.e.) the rites, and the knowledge of the soul, (taught) in this whole ordinance of the Self-existent (*Svayambhu*), which is unknowable and unfathomable.'

4. He, whose power is measureless, being thus asked by the high-minded great sages, duly honoured them, and answered, 'Listen!'

5. This (universe) existed in the shape of Darkness, unperceived, destitute of distinctive marks, unattainable by reasoning, unknowable, wholly immersed, as it were, in deep sleep.

6. Then the divine Self-existent (*Svayambhu*, himself) indiscernible, (but) making (all) this, the great elements and the rest, discernible, appeared with irresistible (creative) power, dispelling the darkness.

---

7. He who can be perceived by the internal organ (alone), who is subtle, indiscernible, and eternal, who contains all created beings and is inconceivable, shone forth of his own (will).

8. He, desiring to produce beings of many kinds from his own body, first with a thought created the waters, and placed his seed in them.

9. That (seed) became a golden egg, in brilliancy equal to the sun; in that (egg) he himself was born as Brahman, the progenitor of the whole world.

16. But, joining minute particles even of those six, which possess measureless power, with particles of himself, he created all beings.

. . . .

---

42. But whatever act is stated (to belong) to (each of) those creatures here below, that I will truly declare to you, as well as their order in respect to birth.

43. Cattle, deer, carnivorous beasts with two rows of teeth, Rakshasas, Pisakas, and men are born from the womb.

44. From eggs are born birds, snakes, crocodiles, fishes, tortoises, as well as similar terrestrial and aquatic (animals).

45. From hot moisture spring stinging and biting insects, lice, flies, bugs, and all other (creatures) of that kind which are produced by heat.

46. All plants, propagated by seed or by slips, grow from shoots; annual plants (are those) which, bearing many flowers and fruits, perish after the ripening of their fruit;

47. (Those trees) which bear fruit without flowers are called vanaspati (lords of the forest); but those which bear both flowers and fruit are called vriksha.

48. But the various plants with many stalks, growing from one or several roots, the different kinds of grasses, the climbing plants and the creepers spring all from seed or from slips.

49. These (plants) which are surrounded by multiform Darkness, the result of their acts (in former existences), possess internal consciousness and experience pleasure and pain.

ANALYSIS:

The first three verses are problematic and throw the reader into a conundrum; the text conflates temporal social laws with notions of Existence and Creation, which are based on the Upanishads. In these introductory verses, a reader, therefore, will get to know the Upanishads in a simpler, accessible form, and at the same time, s/he will also be introduced to the *Varnashrama*, or the caste system; the implication is obvious – both of these are seen on the same spectrum, and having the same kind of truth content when it is obviously not. The text is undoubtedly a skilful work of rhetoric, as two, quite disparate systems are juxtaposed, which do not necessarily have the same degree of absolute truth.

The text of *Manusmriti* works on ideas that have already been referred to in the Upanishads but gives it a completely gendered perspective, and thereby, codifies gender norms. The "divine Self-existent" is defined as "*Svayambhu*, himself" and seen as being male; but in the Upanishads, this same concept of Brahman is referred to as being genderless and addressed as It: for example, in the *Kena Upanishad*, we are told:

We do not know (Brahman to be such and such); hence we are not aware of any process of instructing about It. (Part I; Verse 3)

In the *Upanishads*, the Absolute or Brahman is genderless; and yet, in *Manusmriti*, this same concept is referred to in a distinct, gendered manner.

And the text moves on to talking about creation and atoms ("minute particles") which form creatures and this indeed, is a narrative about creation. Further on, there are parts which read like a class on biology of sorts; and there are concepts of evolution and there is also a bit on classification.

Undoubtedly, there is a need to ensure that such interesting parts of the *Manusmriti* are read and that the reading public is made aware that not everything is problematic in the text; we need to ensure that revised versions are rewritten, which does away with the extremely unconstitutional rhetoric which is intrinsic to the whole notion of the *Varnashrama*, and at the same time, these revised editions of the *Manusmriti* will present us with the core essence of Hinduism, which is a-temporal.

EXTRACTS FROM CHAPTER 3.

15. Twice-born men who, in their folly, wed wives of the low (Sudra) caste, soon degrade their families and their children to the state of Sudras.

16. According to Atri and to (Gautama) the son of Utathya, he who weds a Sudra woman becomes an outcast, according to Saunaka on the birth of a son, and according to Bhrigu he who has (male) offspring from a (Sudra female, alone).

17. A Brahmana who takes a Sudra wife to his bed, will (after death) sink into hell; if he begets a child by her, he will lose the rank of a Brahmana.

18. The manes and the gods will not eat the (offerings) of that man who performs the rites in honour of the gods, of the manes, and of guests chiefly with a (Sudra wife's) assistance, and such (a man) will not go to heaven.

19. For him who drinks the moisture of a Sudra's lips, who is tainted by her breath, and who begets a son on her, no expiation is prescribed.

ANALYSIS:

1. Why exactly should there be such prescriptive behavior ascribed to men and women?

2. The above narrative, which is extremely sex-ist and caste-ist, should be censored; if such texts are disseminated in the public realm, without amendations – as a part of religious discourse – then the text can be construed as stating unconstitutional rhetoric, and violating the Fundamental Rights that are granted to all the citizens of India.

3. Of what relevance are such sections in a text on Hindu *Shastra*? These parts from the *Manusmriti*, should indeed, be erased, and revised versions should be re-written.

4. Thus, the question to ask is: does the text infringe on our fundamental Right to Equality that is guaranteed in the Constitution of India?

SECTION III: EXTRACTS FROM THE *ADHYTAMA RAMAYANA*.[5]

---

[5] All references are from Swami Tapasyananda's *Adhyatma Ramayana*, Sri Ramakrishna Math: Mylapore, Madras (undated).

3 Extracts from RAMA'S MARRIAGE TO SITA in the BALA KANDAM

Rama's Marriage to Sita.

Verses 58-82. Pages: 37-39.

Now that the marriage ceremony was over, Janaka narrated to the sages Vasishtha and Viswamitra, an account about Sita's past, which he happened to hear from Narada. …
'One day while I had withdrawn myself into solitude, there came sage Narada, singing to the accompaniment of his noted Vina, hymns in praise of the all-pervading Narayana. [He said] to me:

> Hear from me a secret that will lead to your welfare.
> For ,the blessing of your devotees, for the
> destruction of Ravana and for the achievement of
> the purposes of the celestials, the Supreme Lord, the

director and master of the senses, has incarnated Himself in a human body, which he has assumed by the power of His Maya. He is born as the son of King Dasaratha as the world-famous Sri Rama. His spiritual counterpart, Yoga-Maya, has manifested Herself in your house. ...

Instructing me thus that celestial sage departed to his divine abode.'

After having praised Rama in this way, King Janaka gave valuable presents to that high-souled one of Raghu's line. He presented him with a hundred crores of gold coins (dinara), a thousand chariots, ten thousand horses, six hundred elephants, a lakh of foot-soldiers and three hundred female attendants. Besides he gave Sita, his dear daughter, valuable clothes and jewellery, resplendent with gems and pearls. After honouring the sages like Vasishtha, the princes Bharata and Lakshmana, as also King Dasaratha according to protocol, King Janaka bade farewell to the Lord of the Raghus. Thereupon, with tears in their eyes the wives of the king embraced their weeping daughter Sita, and adviced her: "O dear one, be devoted to the father and mother of your husband. Be with Rama wherever he is. Observing the duties of a chaste wife (pativrata), live in happiness."

ANALYSIS:

1. The text represents the genre of pastoral literature. We see the contrast between the gifts that are given to Rama and Sita which are very opulent – as befitting royalty -- and these objects become a contrast to the austere life that they would lead in the forest.

2. Narrative methods.

3. In this chapter, the text begins with the idea that Rama is the Supreme Lord, and that he has "incarnated himself in a human body"; this statement is not problematic and what becomes really suspect is the fact that such notions are always juxtaposed with prescriptive social codes of conduct and behavioural norms about how men and women should behave. A recurring trope that occurs in the text is the notion

of the "chaste" wife and that a wife's duty is towards her husband and his family, and yet it is never the other way around where the husband has duties towards his wife's family. The question, thus is, need such texts be disseminated in the public realm − over centuries?

3 Extracts from CONVERSATION BETWEEN RAMA AND NARADA in the AYODHYA KANDAM

Conversation Between Rama and Narada.

Verses: 9-30. Pages: pp 47-49.

Thereupon Narada said to Rama, the lover of all devotees: "O Rama! Why art Thou trying to misguide me by such words, as if Thou wert just a worldly man?

O All-pervading One! Thy statement that Thou art one involved in Samsara is true, indeed, in a way. For, is not Maya, the First Cause of the whole universe, Thy Consort?

It is by Thy mere presence that she generates Brahma and the other offspring of hers. It is with Thee as her support that Maya, constituted of the three Gunas, subsists. It is by Thy support that she constantly gives birth to three types of beings – those that are Sattvika (Sukla or white), Rajasa (Lohita or red) and Tamasa (Krishna or black). ... To put it briefly, whatever female form is there in this universe, that the auspicious Sita is. And whatever male form there is, that Thou art, O scion of the Raghu's line.

...

Pure Consciousness has three adjuncts – gross, subtle and causal. When identified with these, Pure Consciousness is called Jiva, Cosmic or individual, Devoid of them He is the Supreme Lord. O the noblest of Raghu's line! Thou art the Pure Consciousness, the Witness – ... The whole universe has originated from Thee; it remains established in Thee; and it dissolves in Thee.

Therefore, design to bless me, O Lord! and let not Thy Maya delude me."

ANALYSIS:

1. Gender roles are defined in a prescriptive manner; the above statements which refer to the Absolute Divine make that clear. Sri Rama is God incarnate; and it is through his presence and his support that Maya, his Consort, is the First Cause of the Universe.

2. Sri Rama is construed as being Pure Consciousness and the whole Universe as having "originated" from Him. This is undoubtedly, problematic.

3. In the *Kena Upanishad*, Brahman or Pure Consciousness is referred to as "It"; on the other hand, in the *Katha Upanishad*, a shift occurs whereby, Brahman, or realization of Brahman, is seen within a gendered parameter:

"That Purusa indeed, who keeps awake and goes on creating desirable things even when the senses fall asleep, is pure; and He is Brahman, and He is called the Immortal. All the worlds are fixed on Him; none can transcend Him. This indeed is that. (Part II. Canto II. Verse 8)

4 Extracts from PROPOSAL OF INSTALLING RAMA AS YUVARAJA in the AYODHYA KANDAM

Proposal of Installing Rama as Yuvaraja.

Verses: 5-16. Pages: 50-51.

"And get together all the necessary ingredients for installation ceremony. Give information to Rama about this. Let banners and flags of various colours be hoisted on all sides.   Let canopies and other decorations inlaid with gold and pearls be put up."

. . .

In obedience to the King's command, Sumantra in great joy enquired of the sage Vasishtha what he should do in this connection. Thereupon Vasishtha, the greatest among men of knowledge, replied to him:

"Tomorrow early morning, station at the main gate sixteen virgins adorned with ornaments of gold and an elephant also with decorations of gold studded with gems.

A four-tusked elephant of the breed of Airavata has to be got for this, besides numerous golden pots filled with the waters of holy rivers.

You must collect three fresh tiger skins. A ceremonial white umbrella with pearl pendants and a handle studded with gems is also required.

There should be kept ready fragrant garlands, costly garments and exquisite jewellery. Let holy men, well honoured and holding Kusa grass in hand be stationed at the proper place.

In the palace there must be assembled artistes of several kind, dancing girls, musicians, flutists, and experts in the use of various kinds of musical instruments.

Outside the palace regiments of elephants, horses and foot soldiers should stand attention with their arms. The Deities of all the temples in the city should be worshipped with ample offerings. Let vassal kings assemble with various articles of presentation."

[THEN VASISHTHA WENT TO RAMA'S PALACE AND SAID]

Verses: 27-33. Pages: 52-53.

"Though imperceptible to the senses, Thou art the inner pervade of all, and the One who regulates and sustains the progress of the world of Becoming. Thou who art born only out of Thy own accord, hast assumed a body of pure Sattva and hast appeared as man in the world by virtue of Thy Yoga-maya. I know that the profession of priesthood is disreputable. But having known earlier from the words of Brahma that the Supreme Being will be born as Rama in the line of the Ikshvakus, I have, ORama, accepted this ignoble profession of priesthood in order that I may be related to Thee as Thy preceptor.

O Thou, the delight of Raghu's clan! My desire has now been fulfilled. I have now become Thy preceptor (Guru), and if Thou art inclined to pay back the debt that a disciple owes to the Guru, grant that Mahamaya, thy Power, which is under Thy control and which deludes the whole world, may not delude me in that way.

In this particular context I have revealed in Thy presence what I should not do anywhere else."

ANALYSIS:

1. The pomp and ostentatiousness that is associated with life in the palace subsequently becomes a contrast to the stark simple life that the protagonists lead in the forest. The narrative follows the usual structure of a pastoral text.

2. Sri Rama is described as Pure Consciousness (Sattva) and "imperceptible to the senses" and the "One who regulates and sustains the progress of the world of Becoming"; he has been "born only out of" His "own accord" and has "appeared as man in the world by virtue of" His "Yoga-maya." This is a problematic statement as the Upanishads refer to Pure Consciousness/ Brahman as It and being genderless.

3. The *Adhyatma Ramayana,* has to be read as articulating a desire to undo the *Varnashrama;* Vashishtha describes himself in the following manner: "I know that the profession of priesthood is disreputable" and that it was an "ignoble profession," thus drawing attention to the fact that Brahmins could not be necessarily seen as the custodians of Divine Knowledge. The Upanishad-ic tradition is therefore, being critiqued.

4. Gender roles are codified as "Mahamaya" is defined as Sri Rama's "Power" and under His "control" which deluded the "whole world." The readers need to interrogate the need for such gender specific norms.

5 Extracts from OBSTRUCTION OF RAMA'S INSTALLATION in the AYODHYA KANDAM

Obstruction of Rama's Installation.

Verses: 19-22. Page: 60.

[KAIKEYI SPOKE TO KING DASARATHA]:

"The second boon I want is that Rama should be immediately sent into exile to the forest of Dandaka. Let Sri Rama, dressed in an ascetic's garb of tree-bark, wearing matted locks, and devoid of all ornaments, live in the forest, subsisting on roots and fruits, for fourteen years. At the end of that period, let him return to the country or stay on in the forest itself if he prefers to do so. The lotus-eyed Rama should depart to the forest by the next sunrise."

ANALYSIS:

1. The contrast that is made is quite obvious: from the opulence of palace life, Sri Rama has to be sent to exile, dressed in an "ascetic's garb of tree-bark" and with "matted locks" and "devoid of ornaments." The text prepares the readers to begin the journey into the forest and into a life of the nomadic; this is a standard literary technique of the pastoral genre.

6 Extracts from RAMA'S EXILE TO THE FOREST in the AYODHYA KANDAM

Rama's Exile to the forest.

Verses: 75-84. Pages: 73-74.

[SITA INSISTS ON RAMA]

"In my girlhood, a great astrologer, on seeing me, had predicted that I would have to live with my husband in a forest. May that scholar's words come true! I shall certainly go with you.

I shall tell you one thing more, and hearing that, please decide to take me into the forest. I have heard the various versions of the Rama-saga (Ramayana), recited by many scholars. In which of these, do you find Rama going to the forest without Sita? In none, to be sure. Therefore, I have to go with you."

[RAMA AGREED]

"Your necklaces and other jewellery may be given over to our perceptor's wife, Arundhati. We shall go to the forest after giving all our wealth as gift to holy men." Saying so, he asked Lakshman to gather together a large number of pious Brahmans, and he gave them as gift several hundreds of cows and valuable pieces of cloth and ornament. They were all adepts in Vedas, of noble conduct and householders with families. Sita gave away all her important ornaments to Arundhati, while Rama gave much wealth as present to the attendants of his mother. Thus Rama gave numerous gifts to the residents of the palace, to his servants, to the residents of the city

ANALYSIS:

1. The text comments upon itself; this kind of meta commentary allows us to become self-conscious readers. This is a literary device whereby we are made aware of the numerous textual versions that exist, and Sita draws attention by stating that in all the different versions of the *Ramayana*, Sita always accompanies her husband in exile.

2. The act of giving jewelry and his wealth away, whereby the king becomes a pauper in a conscious manner, is a necessary act that accompanies the genre of the pastoral.

7 Extracts from RAMA'S DEPARTURE TO THE FOREST in the AYODHYA KANDAM

Rama's Departure to the Forest.

Verses: 10-16. Page: 75.

When all good men were thus mourning, [at the fact that Rama was leaving the kingdom] the great sage Vamadeva, who was amidst them, came forward to comfort them. He said to them: "Do not be downcast with sorrow, thinking either of Rama or Sita. Listen to what I say regarding the truth about them.

This Rama is none but the Supreme Being – Mahavishnu Adi-Narayana. This Sita, the daughter of Janaka, is Makalakshmi, famous as the Yogamaya of Vishnu. The one whom you know as Lakshmana is Adisesha now following him. The Lord, uniting Himself with Maya, has taken these different forms."

ANALYSIS:

1. Vamdeva, the great sage, reiterates what is the central theme of the *Adhyatma Ramayana*; that Sri Rama was the Supreme Being and Sita, his consort was Yoga-maya. This dichotomy simply reiterates very specific gender roles.

8 Extracts from BHARATA'S RETURN AND AFTER in the AYODHYA KANDAM

Bharata's Return and After.

Verses: 55-67. Page: 111-112.

[Kaikeyi repents]

"O Rama! Under a spell of delusion my evil mind prompted me to obstruct Thy installation as the Yuvaraja. I beseech Thee to pardon me for the bad turn I did to Thee thereby. Forgiveness is the very nature of good men. You are verily Mahavishnu, the Supreme Spirit and Eternal Being, whose nature is not clear to any one. Assuming the form of a man Thou art hiding Thy identity. Man performs good and evil acts only under Thy prompting. This whole world is subject to Thy will, and is without any freedom. Just as puppet dolls dance according to the will of their hidden director who pulls the strings unseen, so is this multiformed Maya a dancer manipulated by Thy will. ...."

Hearing these words of Kaikeyi, Rama said to her smilingly: "O noble lady! What you have just now said is the exact truth. The words that came out of your mouth, took shape under My prompting."

Verses: 76-79. Page: 113-114.

As for Rama, though he took his residence in Chitrakuta with Sita and Lakshmana amidst the settlement of the ascetics of that place, he did not, however, continue to stay there long. For, knowing that Rama was staying at Mount Chitrakuta, large numbers of people from the countryside began to visit that place because of their eagerness to meet him. To avoid the disturbance from the crowds, as also for the fulfilment of the ultimate object of his exile to the forest, he abandoned his residence at Chitrakuta, and proceeded towards Dandakaranya. On the way he along with Sita and his brother, reached the Ashrama of the sage Atri, which was situated at a very solitary place, with the necessary facilities for one to stay all round the year.

ANALYSIS:

1. The pastoral element in the text is predetermined; if Kaikeyi had sent Sri Rama into banishment as a result of Rama's "will" as the "whole world [was] subject to [His] will" like puppets – then one can argue that the protagonist wanted to be sent into exile into the forest and simply used Kaikeyi as a tool.

2. We need to be able to read these elements of the pastoral in this text; how was life amongst the ascetics and the forest dwellers?

9 Extracts from THE MEETING WITH SABARI in the ARANY KANDAM

[The Meeting With Sabari]

Verses: 1-2. Pages: 166-168.

Sabari and her antecedents.

The Gandharva, who was about to depart after getting the Lord's grace, now said to Rama, "O scion of Raghu's line! At a little distance on your way there is an Ashrama where an acsetic woman named Sabari, devoted to the practise of Bhakti, lives, constantly meditating on Thy Feet."

[RAMA VISITS SABARI AT HER ASHRAMA]:

Verses: 11-22.

She said: "O the greatest among the Raghu's! This Ashrams is the place where some great Rishis stayed. For several hundred years, I stayed here attending upon them."… "O Rama! Even the Rishis, my teachers, had not the good fortune of seeing Thee. O Thou immeasurable Being! I am an ignorant and low-born woman. I have not the qualification to be the servant of Thy servants at the hundredth remove"..

Rama said to her in reply: "The state of being a man or a woman, or belonging to a particular class or Ashrama or a state of life, or bearing any special name is not the qualification for my adoration. Devotion is the only adoration."

ANALYSIS:

1. What is the role of Sabari as she is defined as an "ascetic" woman; in the narrative of the *Adhyatma Ramayana*, we come across the different roles that women could perform – from dancing girls to queens.

COMMENTARIES AND NOTES:

This text is a collaboration with:
O₂pen Windows: A Feminist Resource and Research Center.

O₂pen Windows is a feminist research cum *adda* center, based in Bangalore, India. If it could, it would sustain itself with endless cups of tea and lots of stimulating research.

The Purpose: We hope to open up the realm of religious discourse into the public domain of the secular; if we – the people – take these texts into our hands – then, we can do away with those parts that are misogynous and caste-ist and are fundamentally unconstitutional. We, the citizens, need to petition to the government to ensure that religious institutions comply with the laws of the land, and as India is a signatory to CEDAW – the nation complies with it and does not allow any institution (religious or otherwise) to violate it.

www.ingramcontent.com/pod-product-compliance
Lightning Source LLC
Chambersburg PA
CBHW060724030426
42337CB00017B/3009